Searchlight
BOOKS™

What's
Amazing
about Space?

# Exploring
# Exoplanets

Deborah Kops

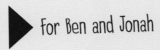 For Ben and Jonah

Lerner Publications Company
A division of Lerner Publishing Group, Inc.
241 First Avenue North
Minneapolis, MN 55401 U.S.A.

Website address: www.lernerbooks.com


Library of Congress Cataloging-in-Publication Data

Kops, Deborah.
        Exploring exoplanets / by Deborah Kops.
            p.    cm. — (Searchlight Books™—What's amazing about space?)
        Includes index.
        ISBN 978-0-7613-5444-4 (lib. bdg. : alk. paper)
            1. Extrasolar planets.  I. Title.  II. Title: Extrasolar exploration.  III. Title: Planets.
        QB820.K67  2012
        523.2'4—dc22                                                          2010046109

Manufactured in the United States of America
1 – DP – 7/15/11

# Contents

# Chapter 1

# STARS AND PLANETS

The sky is filled with stars. On a clear night, you may be able to see lots of them. Planets travel around some of those stars. But you cannot see the planets. Unlike stars, planets do not give off their own light.

This night sky is filled with planets and stars. You can see the stars but not the planets. Do you know why?

A planet is a round object in space that travels around a star. Earth is a planet. The star that Earth travels around is the Sun. Seven other planets travel around the Sun too.

This is what Earth looks like from space. Clouds swirl around Africa and Antarctica in this image.

The Sun and its planets are called the solar system. Planets that travel around other stars are not in our solar system. These planets are called exoplanets. They are very far from Earth.

**This illustration shows the Sun, its planets, and other objects in space.**

## Finding Exoplanets

Astronomers are scientists who study space. For a long time, they thought exoplanets existed. But they had no proof.

Astronomers use giant telescopes to search space for exoplanets.

In the 1990s, astronomers found exoplanets for the first time. They used telescopes to find the planets. Astronomers have discovered more than five hundred exoplanets.

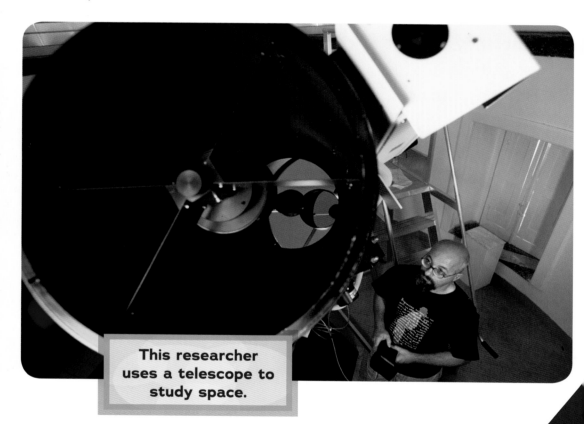

This researcher uses a telescope to study space.

# Chapter 2

# TYPES OF EXOPLANETS

Astronomers look for all kinds of exoplanets. Mostly, they find big ones. Those are the easiest planets to spot. But they also look for small planets that are like Earth.

**This is an artist's idea of what an exoplanet looks like. Can you imagine how other exoplanets might look?**

Astronomers call giant exoplanets Jupiters. The name comes from the planet Jupiter, seen in this photo.

## Jupiters and Neptunes

Jupiter is the largest planet in our solar system. So when astronomers find a very large exoplanet, they call it a Jupiter.

*Hot Jupiter* is the name for a large exoplanet that travels close to its star. Stars are very hot. Planets that travel close to their stars are hot too.

The hot Jupiter in this illustration travels very close to its star.

Some exoplanets are smaller than Jupiter. But they're still much bigger than Earth. These planets are called Neptunes. The real planet Neptune is the fourth-largest planet in our solar system. Some Neptunes get close to their stars. These are called hot Neptunes.

Jupiters and Neptunes are made of gas. The Jupiter and Neptune in our solar system are made of gas too.

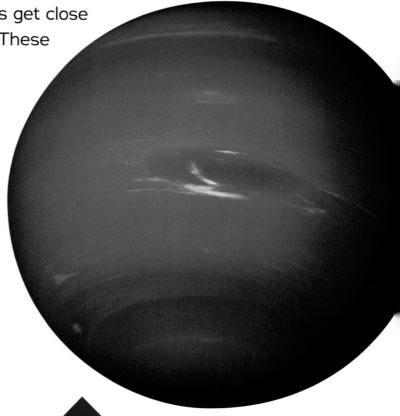

NEPTUNE, SEEN HERE, IS THE SUN'S MOST DISTANT PLANET.

## Earthlike Planets

Smaller, Earthlike planets are usually rocky, just like Earth. But they are very hard to find.

**Astronomers think that the exoplanet in this drawing may be Earthlike.**

Could exoplanets have life on them? Astronomers think an Earthlike planet might. They are excited to learn more about Earthlike exoplanets.

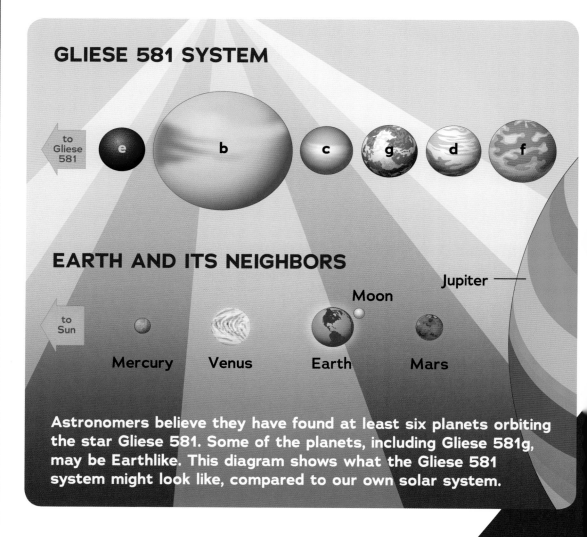

## GLIESE 581 SYSTEM

to Gliese 581

e  b  c  g  d  f

## EARTH AND ITS NEIGHBORS

Jupiter

Moon

to Sun

Mercury  Venus  Earth  Mars

Astronomers believe they have found at least six planets orbiting the star Gliese 581. Some of the planets, including Gliese 581g, may be Earthlike. This diagram shows what the Gliese 581 system might look like, compared to our own solar system.

# Chapter 3

# FINDING EXOPLANETS

Exoplanets are very far from Earth. So we cannot send a spacecraft to look for them. A spacecraft from Earth would take thousands of years to reach them!

The *New Horizons* spacecraft is headed to the farthest parts of our solar system. How long would it take a spacecraft to reach an exoplanet?

We can't actually see most exoplanets, even with telescopes. A star's light is too bright. All we can see is the star. Astronomers must study the star to find out if it has a planet.

These astronomers in New York study the stars. Even the most powerful telescopes can't see most exoplanets.

# The Star That Wobbles

Imagine a telescope is aimed at a star. A big planet travels around the star. The planet and the star tug at each other. A force called gravity makes them do this. The planet's gravity causes the star to wobble a little.

**This artwork shows the outermost exoplanet orbiting the star Gliese 876. The gravity of this big planet causes its star to wobble.**

A telescope can detect the wobble. The wobble tells us that a planet is traveling around the star. This is how scientists have found most exoplanets.

Telescopes must be very sensitive to detect a star's wobble.

This illustration shows a hot Jupiter and its moon orbiting a star.

But there is a problem with this method. Telescopes can easily detect a wobble caused by a big planet. The wobble is much harder to see when a small planet causes it.

## Light That Dips

Wobbles aren't the only thing astronomers look for when they search for exoplanets. Astronomers also look at how these planets affect a star's light.

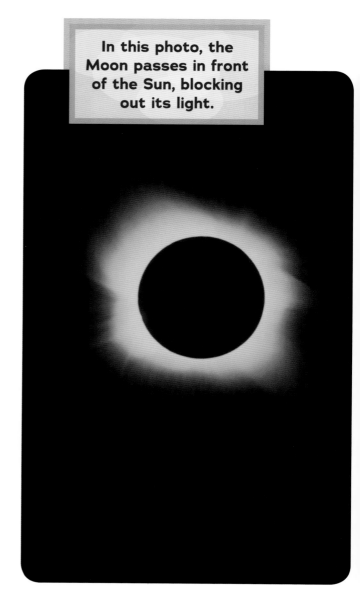

In this photo, the Moon passes in front of the Sun, blocking out its light.

Imagine a distant star. A planet travels around it. As the planet moves around the star, the planet passes between the star and Earth. The planet blocks some of the star's light. The star's light dips just a little. It is not as bright.

This artwork shows the star Gliese 581. The star's light dims a tiny bit as a planet passes in front of it.

Telescopes can detect these small dips in a star's light. An astronomer who finds such a dip might have found an exoplanet. To be sure, the astronomer waits for the planet to pass in front of the star again. Sometimes this takes a few days. Other times, it takes more than a year! Finding exoplanets takes patience.

**Venus passes in front of the Sun in this photo. It blocks some of the light, causing the Sun to appear a tiny bit dimmer.**

# Chapter 4

# PLANET-HUNTING TELESCOPES

A telescope sits on top of a mountain in Chile. The mountain is far from city lights. The telescope has a clear view to the stars.

The European Southern Observatory site is high on a mountain in Chile. Why do astronomers use telescopes far from big cities?

A special instrument is attached to the telescope. It is called the High Accuracy Radial velocity Planet Searcher (HARPS). HARPS helps astronomers search for star wobbles. In 2010, astronomers using HARPS found an Earthlike exoplanet.

**This illustration shows an Earthlike planet discovered by astronomers in Chile.**

The two large telescopes at the W. M. Keck Observatory sit high atop a mountain in Hawaii.

## The Keck Telescope

Astronomers also use the W. M. Keck Observatory to find exoplanets. The observatory has two big telescopes. They sit on a mountain in Hawaii. Each Keck telescope has a giant mirror. The mirrors gather light from the sky.

Earth's atmosphere can get in the telescopes' way. The atmosphere is the air that surrounds Earth. The air moves around and makes stars look as if they are twinkling.

**This photo was taken from space. It shows the Moon through a thin layer of Earth's atmosphere.**

The Keck telescopes' mirrors move too. The mirrors jiggle many times every second. The jiggling mirrors get rid of the twinkle. They give astronomers a clearer view of the stars.

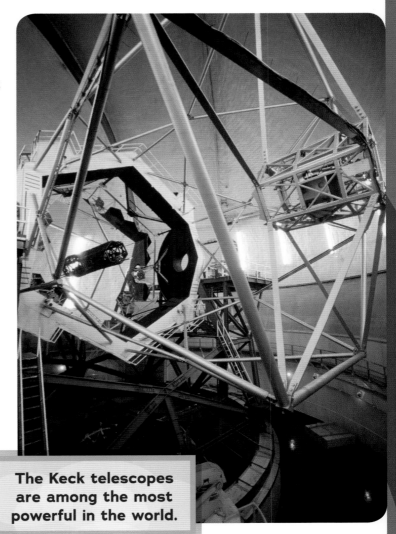

The Keck telescopes are among the most powerful in the world.

## Telescopes in Space

Astronomers also use telescopes in space. Telescopes in space don't have to see through the atmosphere. The Hubble Space Telescope has been in space since 1990. The Hubble took one of the first photos of an exoplanet. The planet is a hot Jupiter.

**The Hubble Space Telescope, seen here in orbit above Earth, has been in space since 1990.**

Another telescope is just for finding Earthlike exoplanets. It is on a spacecraft that circles the Sun, behind planet Earth. The telescope and spacecraft are part of the Kepler Mission.

This rocket blasted off in 2009. It carried the Kepler spacecraft into space.

The Kepler telescope is pointed at a large group of stars. It detects dips in starlight when a planet passes in front of a star. The telescope has found hundreds of exoplanets. At least one is probably an Earthlike planet.

**This drawing shows the Kepler spacecraft circling the Sun as it searches for exoplanets.**

Chapter 5

# THE FUTURE SEARCH FOR EXOPLANETS

The idea of life on an exoplanet excites many scientists. Scientists aren't sure whether life in the universe is common or very rare.

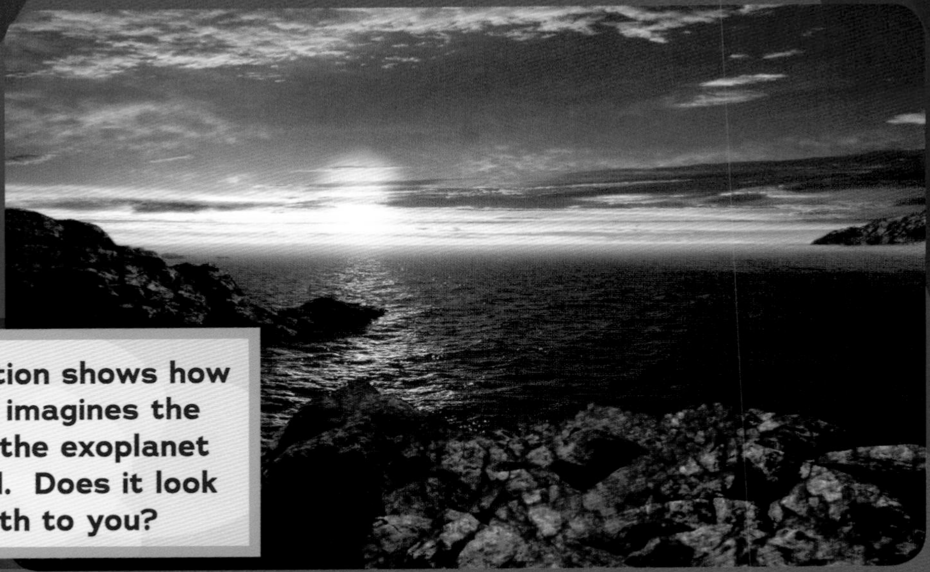

**This illustration shows how one artist imagines the surface of the exoplanet Gliese 581d. Does it look like Earth to you?**

To have life, a planet cannot be too close to its star. The planet will be too hot. But it also cannot be too far away. Then it will be too cold. The planet has to be the right temperature for liquid water to flow. All living things need water.

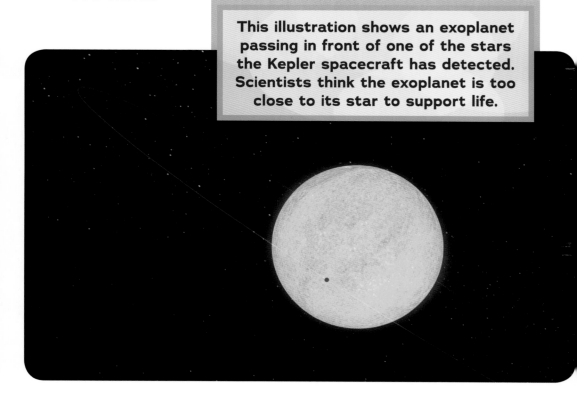

This illustration shows an exoplanet passing in front of one of the stars the Kepler spacecraft has detected. Scientists think the exoplanet is too close to its star to support life.

Astronomers think the Kepler telescope may find this type of planet. New, powerful telescopes in space will join in the search.

THIS ARTWORK SHOWS THE KEPLER SPACECRAFT CIRCLING THE SUN. ITS MISSION IS TO LOOK FOR EXOPLANETS.

## *Gaia* Spacecraft

The *Gaia* spacecraft will make a map of more than a billion stars. *Gaia* will travel around the Sun for five years. During this time, it will record the movement and brightness of each star. It will help scientists build a detailed map of the sky.

The *Gaia* spacecraft's main mission will be to map billions of stars.

A hot Jupiter and asteroids are seen orbiting a star in this artwork. *Gaia* will help scientists determine the size and orbits of exoplanets like this one.

*Gaia* will also observe other objects, including exoplanets. The spacecraft's telescopes will measure the orbits of known exoplanets. It will also help scientists figure out exactly how big the exoplanets are.

## James Webb Science Telescope

The James Webb Science Telescope will look for infrared light. Stars produce infrared light. So do other objects in outer space. We cannot see infrared light. But an infrared telescope can. The James Webb telescope will look for infrared light from exoplanets.

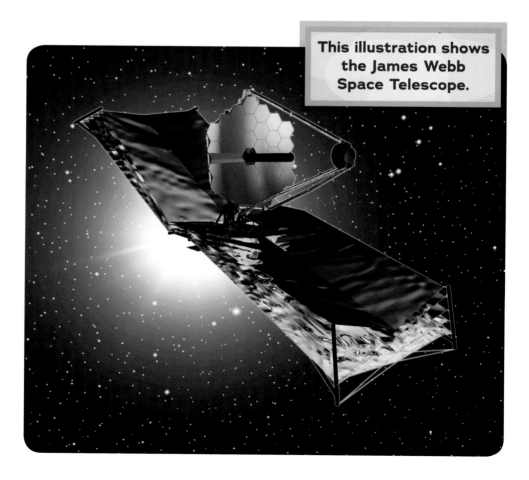

**This illustration shows the James Webb Space Telescope.**

These powerful telescopes will find more and more Earthlike planets. Can scientists tell if any of them have life? Can we find a way to visit the planets? Scientists are looking for answers to these questions. Maybe one day, you can help!

**Stars are forming in this region of space. Could exoplanets be forming there too?**

# Glossary

**astronomer:** a scientist who studies outer space

**atmosphere:** the layer of gas that surrounds Earth

**exoplanet:** a planet that travels around a star other than the Sun

**gravity:** a force that pulls objects together

**infrared:** a type of light that humans cannot see

**Jupiter:** the largest planet in our solar system. *Jupiter* is also the name for exoplanets that are at least as large as the real Jupiter.

**liquid:** a form of matter that can be poured

**Neptune:** the fourth-largest planet in our solar system. *Neptune* is also the name for exoplanets similar in size to Neptune.

**orbit:** the path an object takes as it travels around another object

**planet:** a large, round object in space that travels around a star

**solar system:** the Sun, its eight planets, and the other objects that orbit around it

**telescope:** an instrument that makes faraway objects appear bigger and closer

# Learn More about Exoplanets

## Books

Carson, Mary Kay. *Extreme Planets! Q&A.* New York: HarperCollins, 2008. Learn about the exciting planets in our own solar system as well as about the search for exoplanets.

Hansen, Rosanna. *Jupiter.* Minneapolis: Lerner Publications Company, 2010. Learn more about Jupiter, the gas giant in our own solar system.

Wittenstein, Vicki Oransky. *Planet Hunter: Geoff Marcy and the Search for Other Earths.* Honesdale, PA: Boyds Mills Press, 2010. This short biography tells the story of a man who has helped to discover hundreds of exoplanets.

## Websites

**Cosmic Colors**
http://spaceplace.nasa.gov/en/kids/cosmic/index.shtml#
See what objects in outer space look like through all sorts of different telescopes.

**HowStuffWorks—Planet Hunting**
http://science.howstuffworks.com/planet-hunting.htm
Check out this detailed explanation of how astronomers search for exoplanets.

**Hubblesite**
http://hubblesite.org
Read about the Hubble telescope and see photographs it has taken of outer space.

# Index

# Photo Acknowledgments

The images in this book are used with the permission of: © Oriontrail/Dreamstime.com, p. 4; NASA/JSC, p. 5; © BSIP/Photo Researchers, Inc., p. 6; © Explorer/Photo Researchers, Inc., p. 7; © Pasquale Sorrentino/Photo Researchers, Inc., p. 8; NASA, p. 9; NASA/JPL/Space Science Institute, p. 10; NASA/JPL-Caltech/R. Hurt (SSC), p. 11; NASA/JPL, p. 12; © Detlev van Ravenswaay/Photo Researchers, Inc., pp. 13, 19, 21, 35; © Laura Westlund/Independent Picture Service, p. 14; NASA/JHUAPL/SwRI, p. 15; © Alan Carey/The Image Works, p. 16; © Mark Garlick/Photo Researchers, Inc., p. 17; © National Geographic/SuperStock, p. 18; © Bruce Herman/Stone/Getty Images, p. 20; © Jean Ayissi/AFP/Getty Images, p. 22; © David Nunuk/Photo Researchers, Inc., p. 23; © Martin Bernetti/AFP/Getty Images, p. 24; © David Lloyd/Dreamstime.com, p. 25; © CORBIS, p. 26; © Hank Morgan/Photo Researchers, Inc., p. 27; NASA/JSC, p. 28; NASA/Regina Mitchell-Ryall, Tom Farrar, p. 29; © Dr. Seth Shostak/Photo Researchers, Inc., p. 30; © Ron Miller, p. 31; NASA/Kepler Mission/Dana Berry, p. 32; NASA/Ames/JPL-Caltech, p. 33; © ESA - C. Carreau, p. 34; Courtesy of TRW, p. 36; © European Southern Observatory/Photo Researchers, Inc., p. 37. Front cover: ESA/NASA/UCL (G. Tinetti).

Main body text set in Adrianna Regular 14/20.
Typeface provided by Chank.